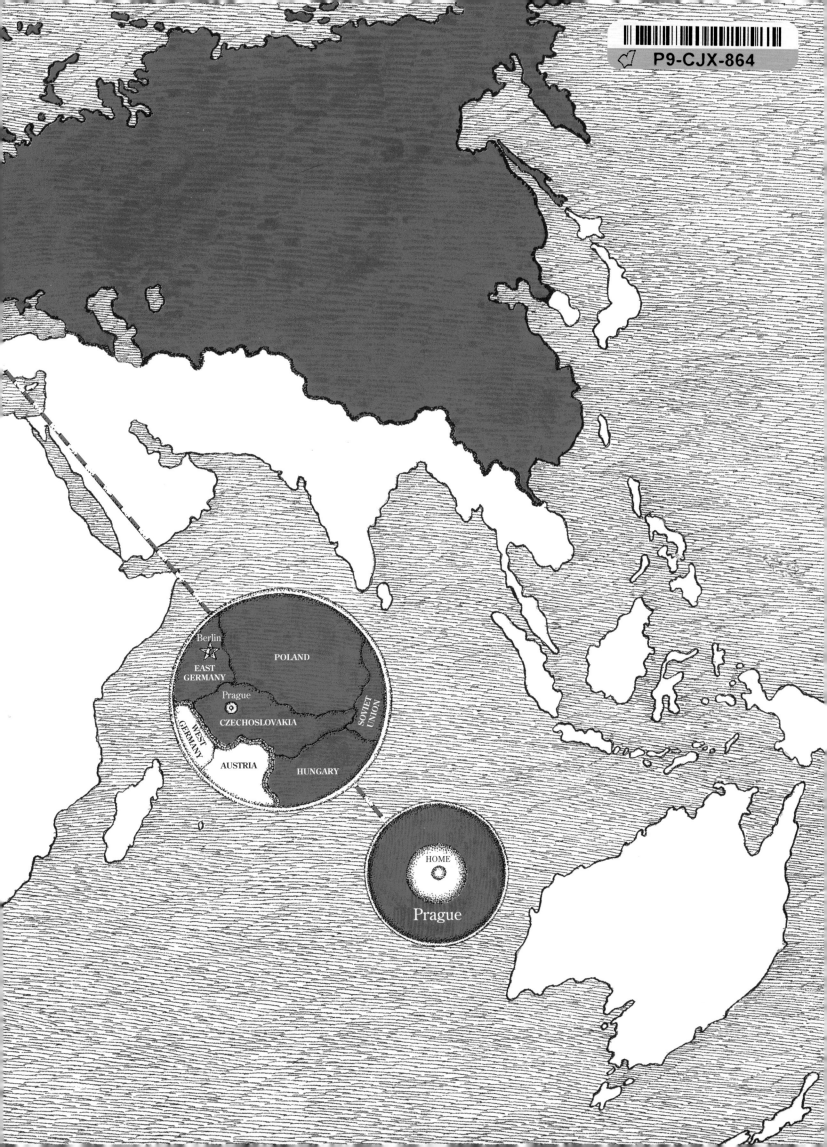

Berlin

POLAND

EAST
GERMANY

Prague

SOVIET
UNION

CZECHOSLOVAKIA

WEST
GERMANY

AUSTRIA

HUNGARY

HOME

Prague

THE
WALL

GROWING UP BEHIND
THE IRON CURTAIN

PETER SÍS

LABYRINT / RAKETA / PRAHA

INTRODUCTION

We don't have to go far back in time to see that the map of the world keeps changing. In the twentieth century alone, the changes were often cataclysmic. In 1917, the Russian Empire was swept by a revolution that brought the Communist Party to power and established the Soviet Union. At the end of World War I in 1918, the Austro-Hungarian Empire fell apart and several countries gained independence. Czechoslovakia was one of them. But after two decades of democracy, Czechoslovakia was taken over by Nazi Germany. Then, in 1939, World War II erupted. The Allies—the United States, Britain, France, and the Soviet Union—defeated Germany and Japan in 1945 and liberated the countries that Germany had occupied. After the war, responsibility for governing these countries was divided between the Allied forces. Most of eastern Europe and the eastern part of Germany fell under Russian control and became known as the Eastern Bloc. The rest of Germany was in the Western Bloc, led by the United States. The Soviet Union and the Western nations managed their territories in very different ways. The Western Bloc countries were all independent democracies, while the Eastern Bloc was tightly controlled by the Soviet Union. But not everyone in the Eastern Bloc countries wanted to live under totalitarian dictatorships, and many people began leaving for the West. To prevent a mass exodus, the Soviet Union fortified the borders around much of Eastern Europe and eventually built a wall that cut the city of Berlin in half. And so Europe was divided—symbolically, ideologically, and physically—by what Winston Churchill, the British statesman, called an Iron Curtain. By the 1950s, the United States and the Soviet Union each had nuclear weapons, but both sides knew that using them to fight another war would be devastating, and for the next forty years the two superpowers coexisted in a tense standoff, avoiding all-out war. This period was called the Cold War. It lasted until the Berlin Wall fell and the Soviet Empire collapsed. I was born at the beginning of it all, on the Red side—the Communist side—of the Iron Curtain.

—P.S.

THE WALL
GROWING UP BEHIND THE IRON CURTAIN
Copyright © 2007 by Peter Sís
All rights reserved
This edition © 2008 by Labyrint

Published by arrangement with Farrar, Straus & Giroux, New York

Published by RAKETA, an imprint of LABYRINT
Dittrichova 5, 120 00 Praha 2
e-mail: labyrint@labyrint.net
Printed in the Czech Republic

1ˢᵗ English edition in the Czech Republic (reprint 2017)

www.labyrint.net

ISBN 978-80-86803-13-5

"This is a special day! I'm taking you to your first rock concert!"

"I went to see this same rock band almost forty years ago!"

"Dad, how come they keep on giving concerts all these years?"

"The one I went to didn't end well…" "Why didn't it?"

"It's a long story. I would have to tell you about a certain boy…"

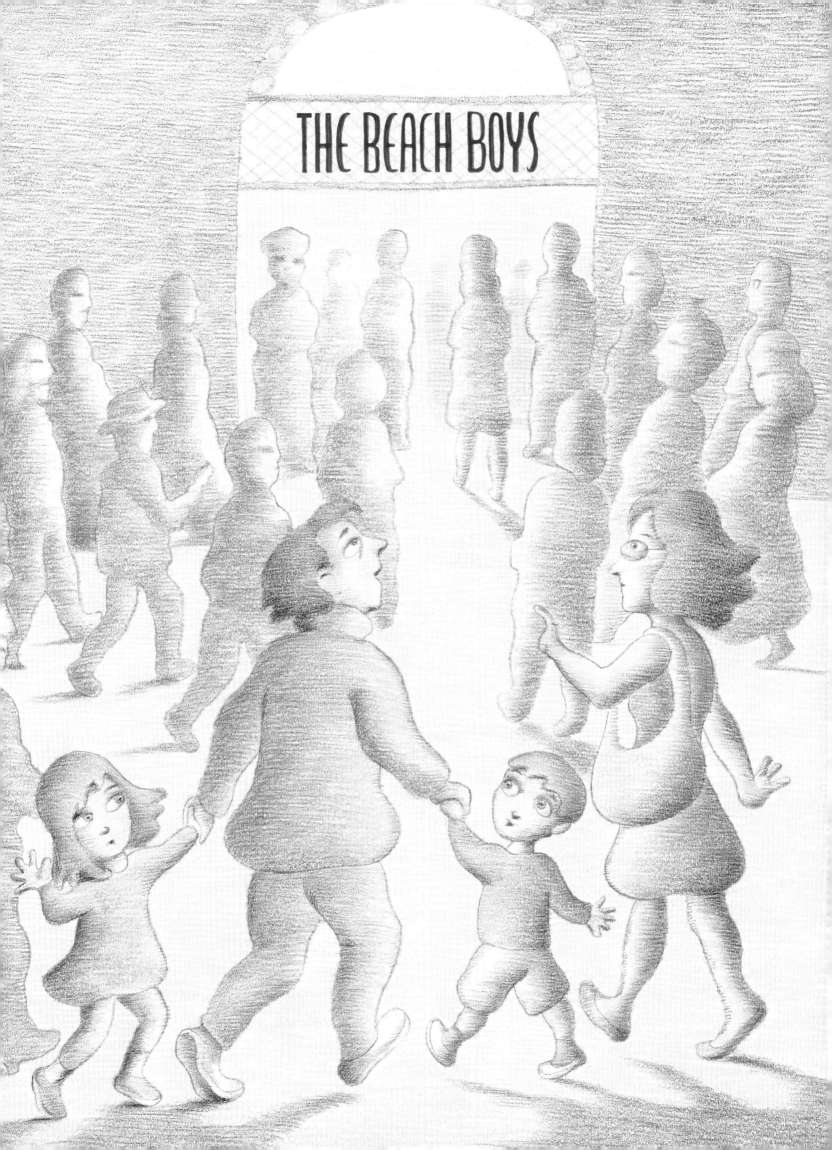

*1948.
The Soviets take
control of
Czechoslovakia
and close the
borders.*

*The People's
Militia enforces
the new order.*

At first he drew shapes.

Communist symbols and monuments appear everywhere.

The Czech government takes its orders from Moscow.

The display of red flags on state holidays— **COMPULSORY.** *People who don't comply are punished.*

Then he drew people.

The Communists take control of the schools.

Russian-language classes— **COMPULSORY.**

Joining the Young Pioneers, the Communist youth movement— **COMPULSORY.**

Political indoctrination— **COMPULSORY.**

Collecting scrap metal— **COMPULSORY.**

First of May parade celebrating the workers of the world— **COMPULSORY.**

After drawing whatever he wanted to at home,

Public displays of loyalty— **COMPULSORY.**

The practice of religion— **DISCOURAGED.**

Children are encouraged to report on their families and fellow students. Parents learn to keep their opinions to themselves.

Citizens participate in the Spartakiad—a mass gymnastics exercise glorifying individual subordination to socialist ideals— **COMPULSORY.**

he drew what he was told to at school.

Hungary 1956. A popular uprising is crushed by the Soviet Union.

Germany 1961. The Berlin Wall is erected by the Soviets to keep East Berliners from defecting to the West. It cuts the city in half.

The Iron Curtain separating East and West is strengthened, and the Cold War escalates.

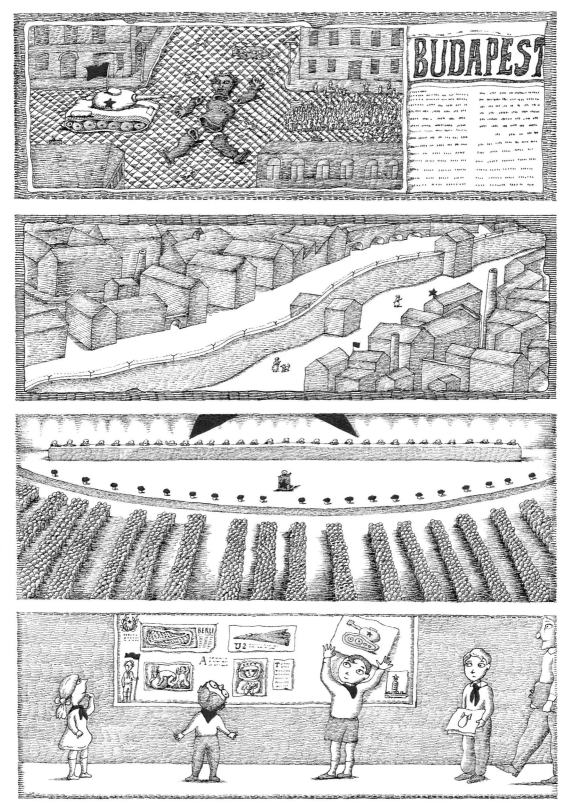

He drew tanks.

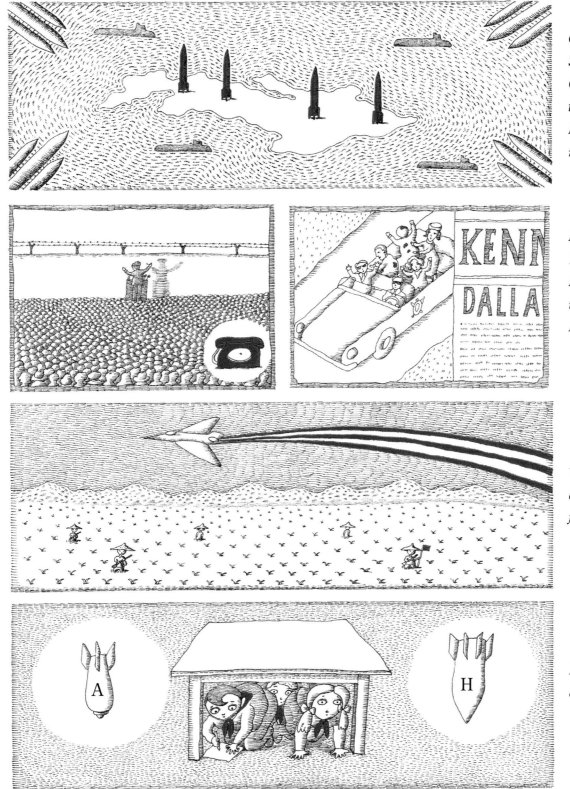

October 1962. Soviet missiles in Cuba are aimed at the United States. Nuclear war is narrowly averted.

June 26, 1963. President John F. Kennedy visits the Berlin Wall and declares, "Ich bin ein Berliner— I am a Berliner."

November 22, 1963. President Kennedy is assassinated in Dallas, Texas.

The United States and Communists fight in Vietnam.

Nuclear war is a constant threat.

He drew wars.

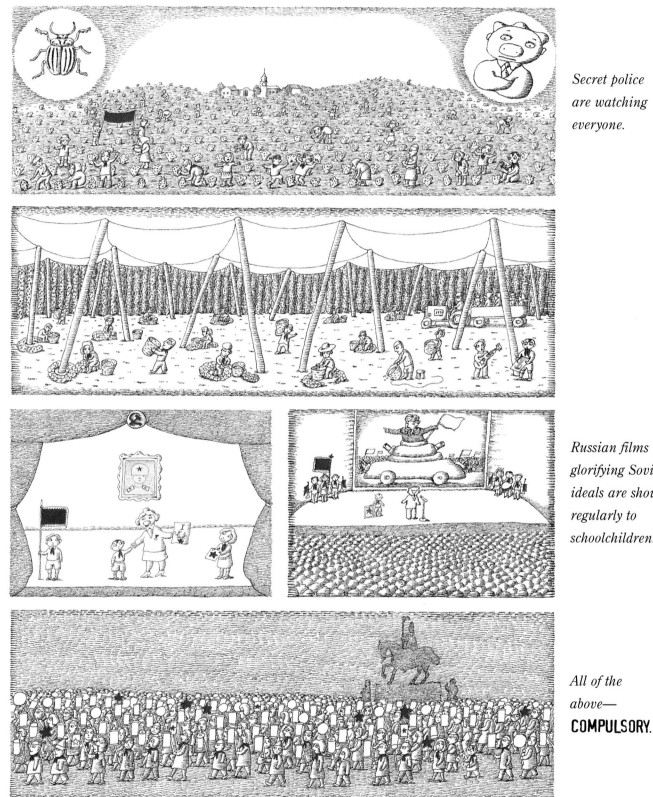

Czechoslovak students help farmers fight a potato beetle infestation. The beetles are blamed on the U.S.A.

Secret police are watching everyone.

Students harvest hops (used for brewing beer).

Russian films glorifying Soviet ideals are shown regularly to schoolchildren.

The Great Socialistic October Revolution is celebrated annually on November 7 by a nighttime march.

All of the above— **COMPULSORY.**

He didn't question what he was being told.

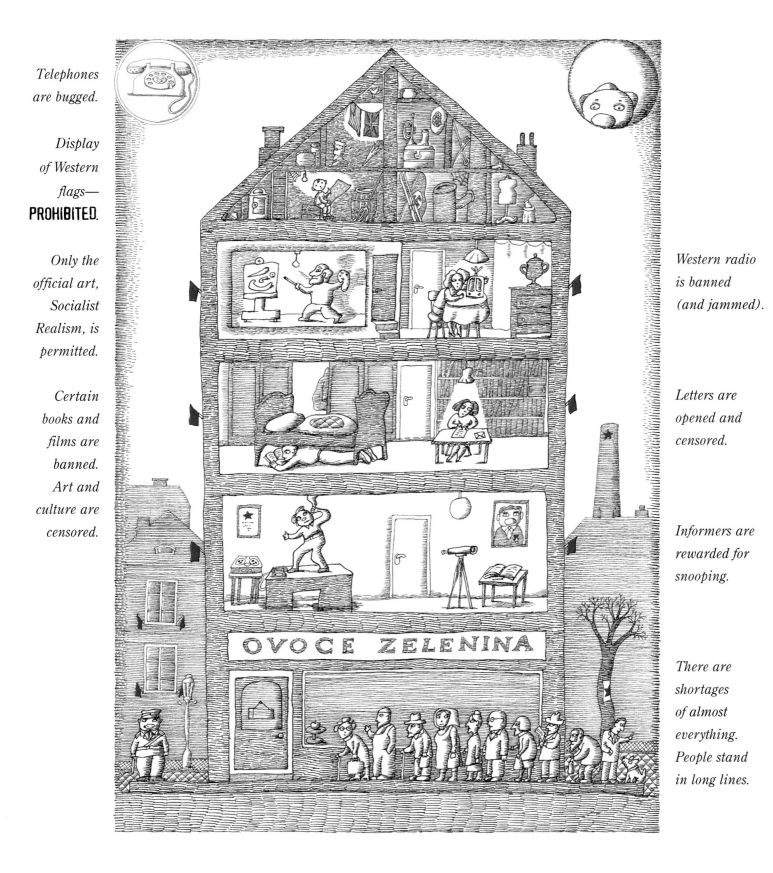

Then he found out there were things he wasn't told.

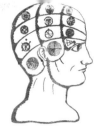

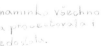

FROM MY JOURNALS

1954

My father has been drafted into the Army Film Unit. They sent him to China to make a film.

We're supporting world peace by not eating meat on Thursdays.

We are all encouraged to get a pen pal in the Soviet Union. I've chosen Volodja in Leningrad. Our letters are graded.

April 1956

My father's cousin Lamin is in prison as an enemy of the state. My grandmother talks to my parents about it in German so my sister and I won't understand. But we understand some of it. He was on a national volleyball team that was going to a tournament in the West, and the players were all planning to stay there. The secret police found out. Lamin is twenty years old and will be in prison for the rest of his life.

February 1957

We went on a skiing vacation in the mountains on the western border. Soldiers with dogs came through the train looking for "subversives" trying to cross the border. The soldiers checked our skis and told us if we saw anyone who looked suspicious or behaved strangely, we should tell. When we got off the train, there were two extra pairs of skis, and two people were missing!

November 3, 1957

The Soviet Union launched a rocket carrying a little dog named Laika into space. I wonder how the dog is going to land?

1958

We were given our Young Pioneer scarves at the Lenin Museum in Prague—all except Dežo Hlaváč because he is from a Gypsy family with "too many children" and is not considered ready.

March 1959

There is a story in our schoolbook about a Russian man who is a class enemy. He hides his wheat harvest in his cellar instead of giving it to the village cooperative. His son, who is a Young Pioneer, finds out and reports it. The family kills the boy. His name is Pavka Morozov. He is a hero. We are told that if we see our parents doing wrong, we should report them.

June 1960

We are rehearsing for the Spartakiad. I'm in the ten-to-twelve-year-old group. Our part is called "Joyous Spring." We wear green shorts and yellow shirts. Each age group has its own segment and different uniform colors. The women are spectacular, and the soldiers are the most daring.

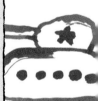

1961
We watch an American movie called
On the Bowery at school. It shows poor
people sleeping in the street. We're told this
is how people in a capitalist country live.

April 12, 1961
The Soviet Union launched the first man
into space, Yuri Gagarin. When he returned,
he landed safely in Siberia.

April 28, 1961
We welcome cosmonaut Yuri Gagarin
to Prague. I wish he had brought his dog
Laika with him.

June 17, 1962
The Czechoslovak National Soccer Team
plays Brazil in the World Cup soccer
championship final in Chile. We lose.

November 1962
Every May we stand guard at the giant Stalin
statue. But now the statue has been blown
up. We will stand guard at the smaller
monuments…

There is a five-year plan for the whole
country. We are building socialism. America
is a capitalist country. So are France, Britain,
Italy, and Holland. But my schoolbook tells
me that America is the most capitalistic and
decadent of all.

The very best Young Pioneers from all
the socialist countries are invited to a camp
in the Soviet Union called Artek.

I took first place in the Historical Museum
Drawing Competition.

September 1963
Colonel Jan Pixa was named a Hero of the
Czech Socialist Republic—for his ingenious
plan for catching "disturbers of the border,"
people trying to cross over to the West.
He made a fake border so the "bad guys"
would think they had gotten through.
When they saw the American flag and were
greeted by secret service men disguised
as American soldiers, they'd think they had
reached the West. The defectors would tell
the secret service everything they knew and
name their friends. What a surprise when
the defectors found out they weren't in the
West after all and were going to prison
for life. Colonel Pixa is a hero.

I built a scooter that collapsed when my
sister, Hana, was riding it downhill.
She hates me!

My school visited the Mausoleum to view
the embalmed body of the first working-class
Communist President of Czechoslovakia,
Comrade Klement Gottwald.
It was scary.

Bits and pieces of news from the West begin to slip through the Iron Curtain.

The Beatles! (Which one is which?)

Elvis, the Rolling Stones, Radio Luxembourg… We secretly tape songs.

Everything from the West seems colorful and desirable.

Citizens age fifteen and over must carry a photo I.D. at all times— **COMPULSORY.**

Slowly he started to question. He painted what he wanted to—in secret.

*There are
no records,
no instruments,
no stylish clothes.
We have to make
and invent
everything.
We all want
to be Beatles.*

*We make our
own shoes,
shades, electric
guitars…*

*Long hair
is a sign of
Western
decadence.
Police have
orders to
cut it.*

*Rock music
is against
the principles
of Socialist art.*

He joined a rock group and painted music.

*January 1968.
The new head
of the
Communist
government,
Alexander
Dubček,
has good
intentions.*

*Slowly, our
world begins to
open up.*

*Censorship
is lifted.*

*The old guard
and the police
are nervous.*

Everything seemed possible . . .

It was the Prague Spring of 1968!

The Beatles

film

Harlem GlobeTroTTers

THeaTer

aLLen GINSBerG

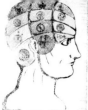

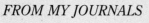

FROM MY JOURNALS

March 1965

I take a walk by the river in the falling snow
and pass a black man with a smiley face.
He nods. Later, I see a poster and realize
I've seen Louis Armstrong, Satchmo.
He's in Prague to give a concert!

May 1965

Allen Ginsberg, the American beat poet,
comes to Prague. Students make him our
Kral Majales (King of May). Then the secret
police accuse him of subversion and deport
him.

August 1965

A U.S. college all-star basketball team plays
in Prague. The best players are some twins
and Bill Bradley.

November 1965

The Party newspaper mentions this wild
woman called Elvis Presley. It turns out
she's a he.

March 1966

My dad came back from France with a 45
single by the Beatles—"A Hard Day's Night."

May 1966

A group of guys with long hair meet in front
of the National Museum and get chased by
the police. When they are caught, the police
pull out scissors and give them haircuts.

Summer 1966

I'm trying to let my hair grow, which is not
appreciated at home or at school. My friends
and I are learning about the Rolling Stones,
Fats Domino, Chuck Berry, rock 'n' roll.
More music, records, and tapes become
available. The Harlem Globetrotters are
coming to Prague.

December 1966

At first blue jeans are permitted as a uniform
of the working classes (but only people with
relatives in the West or those with hard
currency who can shop in the special store
TUZEX are lucky enough to have them).
Then the government changes its mind.
Jeans are a sign of Western decadence.

February 1967

I form a rock group with my friends, but we
have no instruments and we haven't settled
on a name yet.
My father makes me get a haircut. I paint
people with long hair.

May 1967

We start making instruments. It's hard
to make an electric guitar. You plug it into
the radio and it blows a fuse.

June 1967

We play songs by the Rolling Stones, Them,
Small Faces, the Troggs. My friend Zdeněk
is an amazing guitarist.

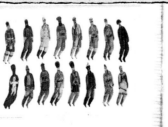

August 1967

Hop-picking time again—a good way to meet girls. After working all day, we get together and sing Beatles songs.

September 1967

There's a rumor that travel restrictions will be lifted. If I can get an invitation from a family in England or Western Europe, I can apply for a passport.

I've written to the *Record Mirror,* a magazine in London that has a pen pal column. I sent a photo and a list of my favorite groups.

October 1967

Our group, which we've named New Force, gives a concert at the Central Puppet Theater. The stage is so small there is no room for the drummer. I meet Alena. I need boots with heels. Expensive! (Get money from Grandma?)

November 1967

A date with Alena. We walk up and down Wenceslaus Square.

I draw comics for the school magazine, like those I've seen from San Francisco. Make posters for a rock club called Olympic. Hurray!

January 1968

Dubček elected First Secretary of the Party. Gives a speech about freedom!

February 1968

Hundreds of letters arrive from *Record Mirror* pen pals…Have to write back, many letters a week…Get map of Europe… Hitchhike? The only way to do it.

March 1968

A rally for Dubček! We all march. He is calling for "socialism with a human face."

May 1968

Censorship is lifted! We can have long hair and wear jeans! But our school magazine is shut down. The principal complains of anarchy.

June 1968

I've learned how to tie-dye shirts and am getting pretty good at it. I tie-dye everything I can get my hands on. The government archives are being opened. I was never told that my uncle Vladimir died in the Communist Leopoldov Prison. The guards killed him. My parents kept this news from us kids. We hold a poetry slam at school on the main staircase! I have my passport with permission to travel to the West. Yippee! I'll go by train to Paris, cross the Channel, hitchhike to London and Liverpool…meet the Beatles? The Soviet Union is planning big maneuvers all over Czechoslovakia this summer.

Summer 1968

I'm leaving for England! Back in August with records and posters and pictures…

August 21, 1968. 500,000 troops from the Soviet Union, Bulgaria, East Germany, Hungary, and Poland invade Czechoslovakia.

Ordinary citizens try to persuade the invading soldiers to leave. They change street signs to confuse them.

The Czech progressive government is sent to Moscow for "reeducation."

Help from the West doesn't come.

Then—it was all over.

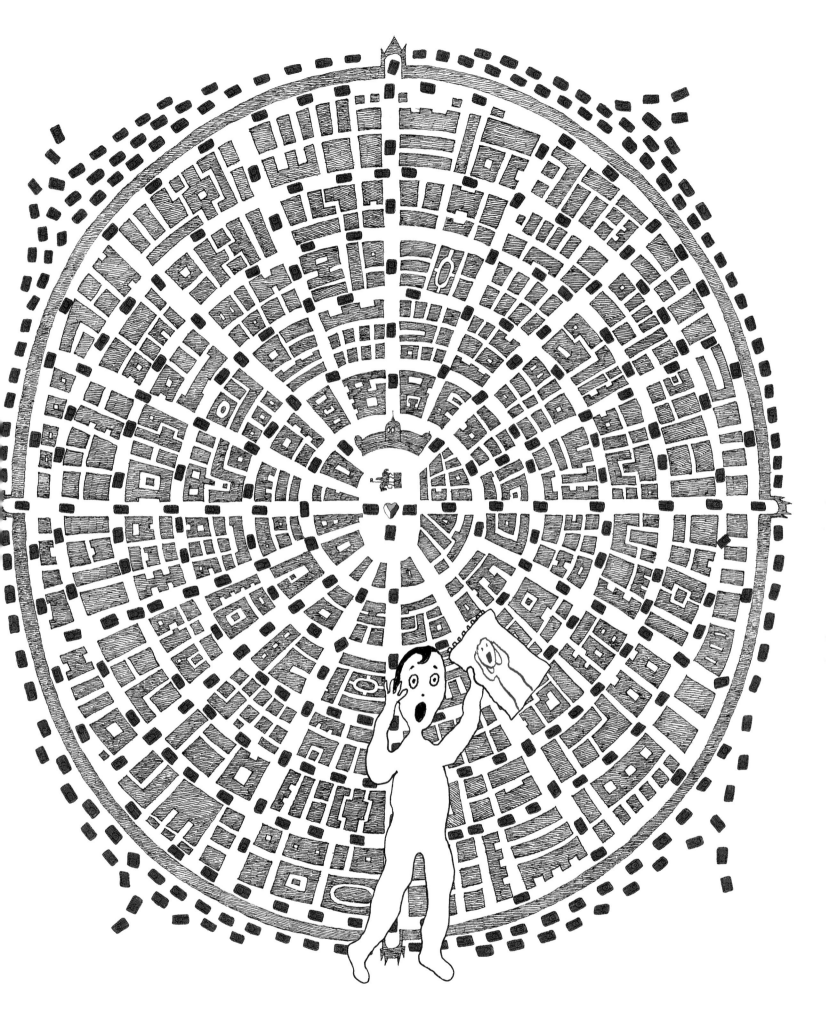

Russian tanks were everywhere.

Ten months after the Soviet invasion, the Beach Boys are invited to Czechoslovakia to give rock concerts.

Rock music fans will be together under one roof.

But out of the dark came a glimmer of hope.

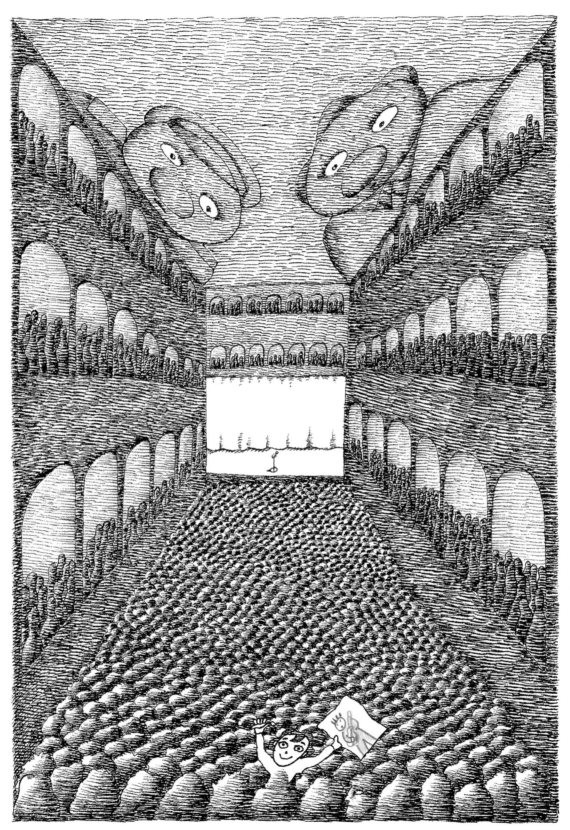

June 17, 1969. The Prague concert takes place in Lucerna Hall.

Police with dogs wait nearby.

The Beach Boys arrived. America to the rescue!

He was painting dreams…

and then nightmares.

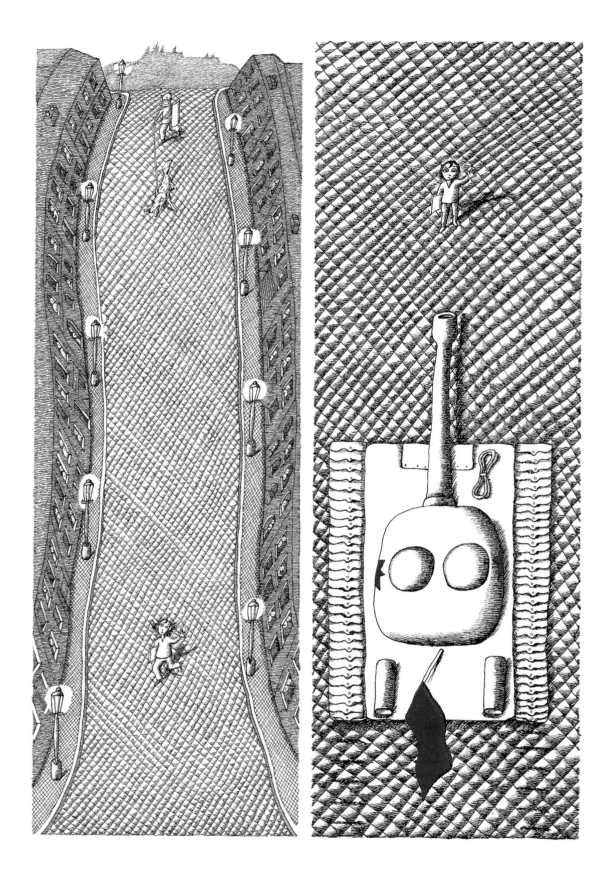

The dreams could be kept to himself,

Anyone considered a threat to the new order is interrogated.

but the drawings could be used against him.

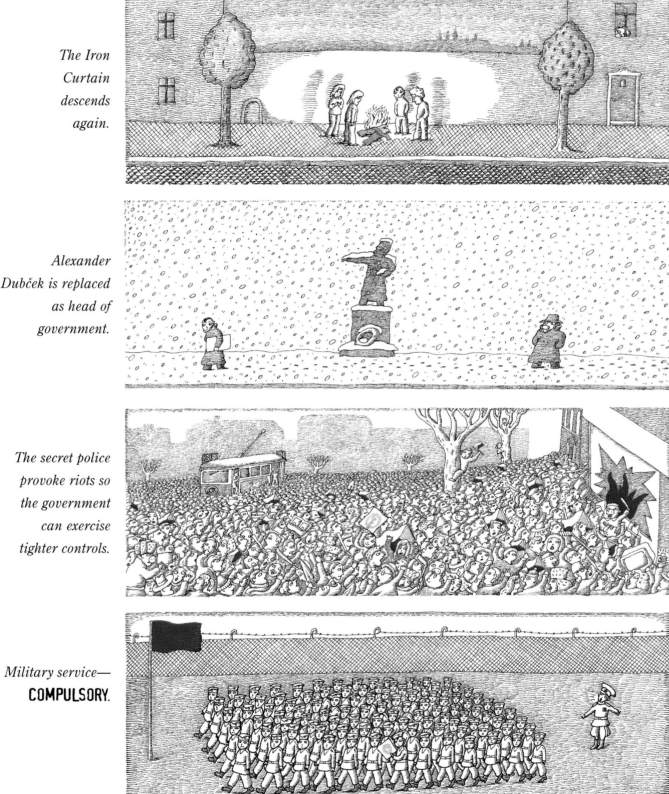

The Iron Curtain descends again.

Alexander Dubček is replaced as head of government.

The secret police provoke riots so the government can exercise tighter controls.

Military service— **COMPULSORY.**

He stopped drawing and was left with only his dreams.

Phones are bugged again, mail opened, people watched.

Western-style art is banned again. Free radio stations are jammed again.

Banned books are secretly translated, copied, and circulated as samizdat.

Discotheques are a new source of information about popular culture.

But he had to draw. Sharing the dreams gave him hope.

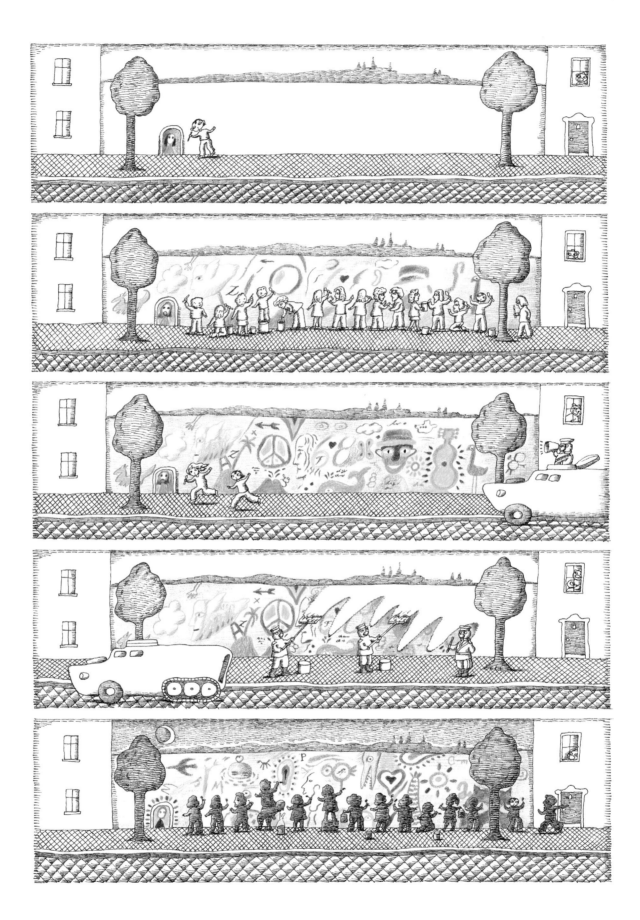

Everyone wanted to draw. They painted a wall filled with their dreams…

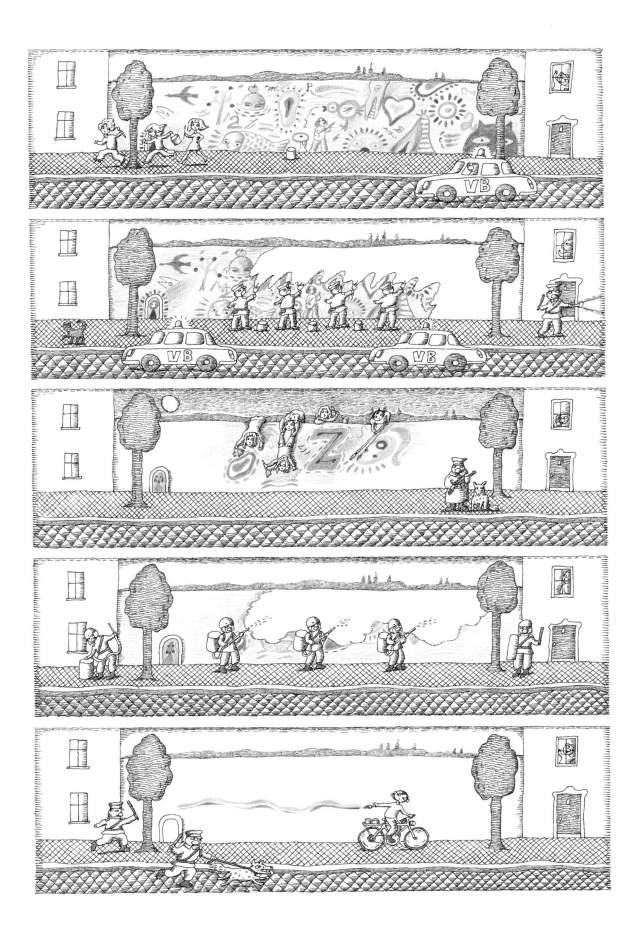

and repainted it again and again.

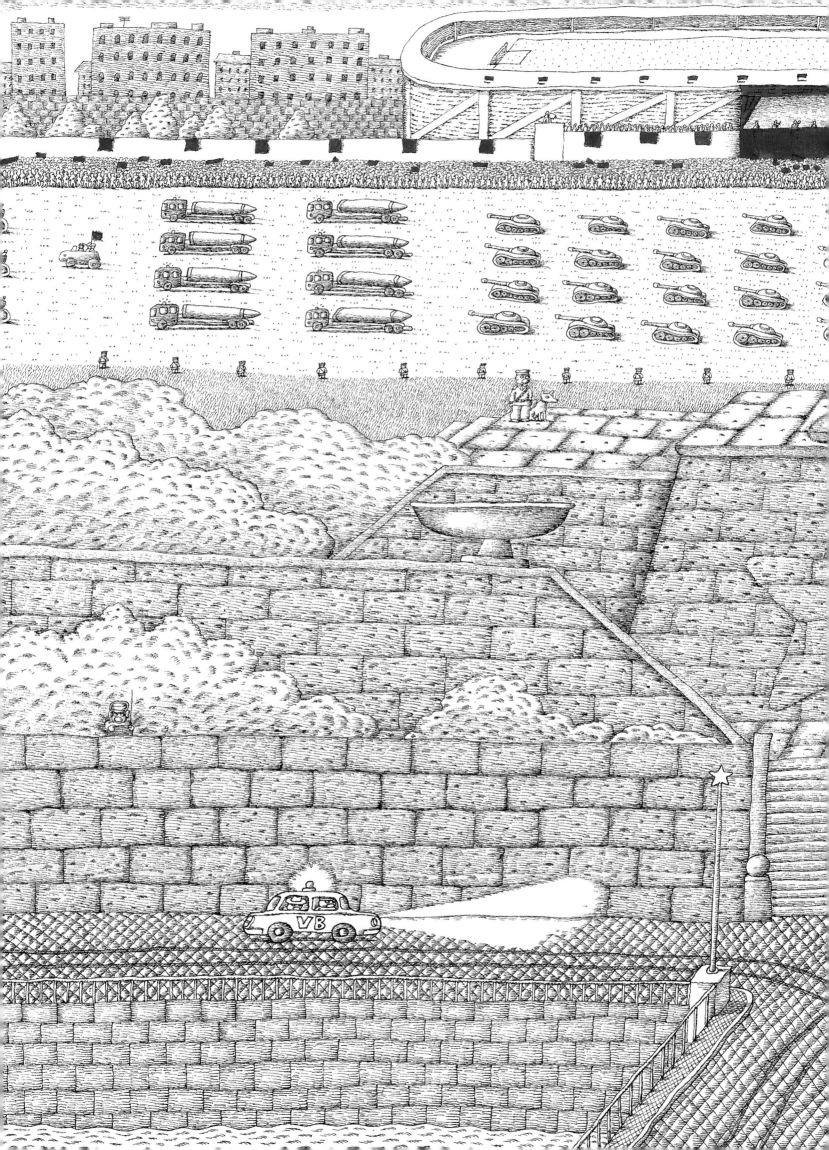

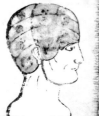

FROM MY JOURNALS

January–February 1969
Jan Palach and Jan Zajíc, students, set themselves on fire to "wake up the nation from lethargy."

1970
Větvička, a fun guy and bass player, died of head injuries after the police beat him in the melee following the Beach Boys concert.

1971
My professor at the Academy of Applied Arts, Adolf Hoffmeister (who wrote *Brundibár*), is stripped of his professorship. Anyone considered progressive is replaced.

1972
The border has closed again. Travel is impossible. Goodbye, swinging London!

June 8, 1972
A group of young people with long hair—I know them well—hijack a plane to West Germany. They shoot the pilot with a gun hidden in a baby's diaper.

February 1973
Every one of us in the academy has to create a piece of art celebrating the Soviet Army. I'm glad I'm in the animation department! I'll just paint the backgrounds and explain that the tanks are coming later.

1974
Graduation…We're told that our generation is not to be trusted and has no future because we are "tainted" by the events of 1968.
To get a permit to have a studio in my own house, I have to prove that I am an artist in good "social standing," that is, a member of the Communist Party. The curious thing is that I have just been offered a position as an assistant professor in the academy. I am told I am the youngest ever to be considered. I am elated, but then comes the condition: I must join the Party. They promise me that no one has to know about it! Thanks, but no thanks. I draw small pictures. I do not need a studio.

1975
My first professional assignment—an album cover for Karel Černoch's *Letiště (Airport)*. I paint a little airport with a red-and-white wind sock blowing in the wind. "Did you check which direction the wind sock is blowing?" the art director asks. I laugh, thinking he's joking. "It's very important," he says, "an ideological issue." If the wind is blowing from west to east, it could be read as coming from West Germany to the Soviet Union. Ideological diversion. Infiltration. He calls the Ministries of Culture and the Interior. We wait for them to call back. "You're in luck!" says the art director. "Your wind is blowing in the right direction."

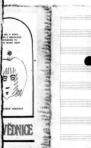

1975–76

Army service.
Rock bands can no longer perform without
a permit.
All artists now have to prove their social
and political qualifications.

1976

The Plastic People of the Universe rock band
are in prison. I used to argue with them,
and do not care for their music—but prison?

January 1977

Dissidents formed an organization called
Charter 77. As a result, some of them are
in prison. Some have been threatened and
tortured, stripped of citizenship, and driven
with their families to the western border
and kicked out of the country.

January 28, 1977

Prominent artists, writers, film directors,
actors, and musicians were invited to the
National Theater for a "celebration."
When they were all in the theater, the doors
were locked, and they were instructed
to sign a document supporting the "fraternal
help of the Soviet Army" in 1968 (that is,
the invasion). Most signed.
Bad news/good news—my dad is in the
hospital. He couldn't attend. I'm almost sure
he wouldn't have signed…What would
I have done?

May 1977

Finally, my first professional film:
an animated fairy tale, *Island for 6,000 Alarm
Clocks* by Miloš Macourek. The story:
6,000 alarm clocks feel beaten down
and unappreciated and walk off the job.
They walk and walk until they get to a little
island where they can ring as they please.
I spend a year painting, cutting,
animating. The film looks great, all ten
minutes of it. Everyone congratulates me.
Then the censors decide that the film gives
the wrong message by suggesting that you
can walk away if you don't like something.
Was I telling people to emigrate? People
are always looking for hidden messages.
There is a whole science to learn about
dealing with censors. You have to give them
something to change. For instance, if you're
making a film or a painting, or writing
a book or a song, you put in a big church.
You can be sure the censors will tell you
to take it out, and perhaps they won't notice
the smaller, important things. Theater
people have the "little white dog" theory.
If you let a little white dog parade across
the front of the stage, the censors won't
notice what is happening in the background.

June 1977

Rumors, rumors, rumors. Everyone
suspects everyone else of being an informer.
Can we hope things are ever going
to get better?

Very few dare to stand up and criticize the government.

Jan Palach protests the regime.

Dissident playwright
Václav Havel is jailed.

Everyone has to prove loyalty to the Soviet system.

Things got worse…

Artists are brought to the National Theater under false pretenses.

Dissidents are forced to do menial jobs.

A doctor

A professor

People are followed, monitored, harassed, imprisoned, deported, and tortured.

and worse.

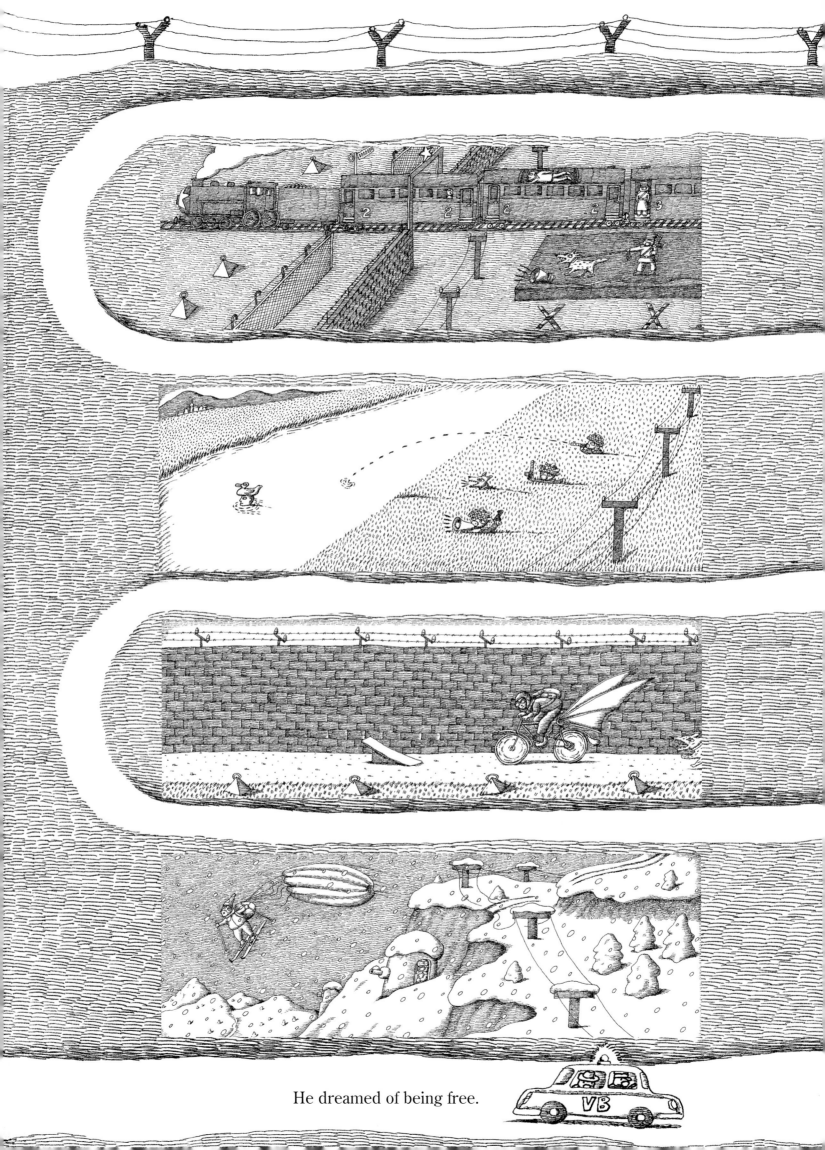

He dreamed of being free.

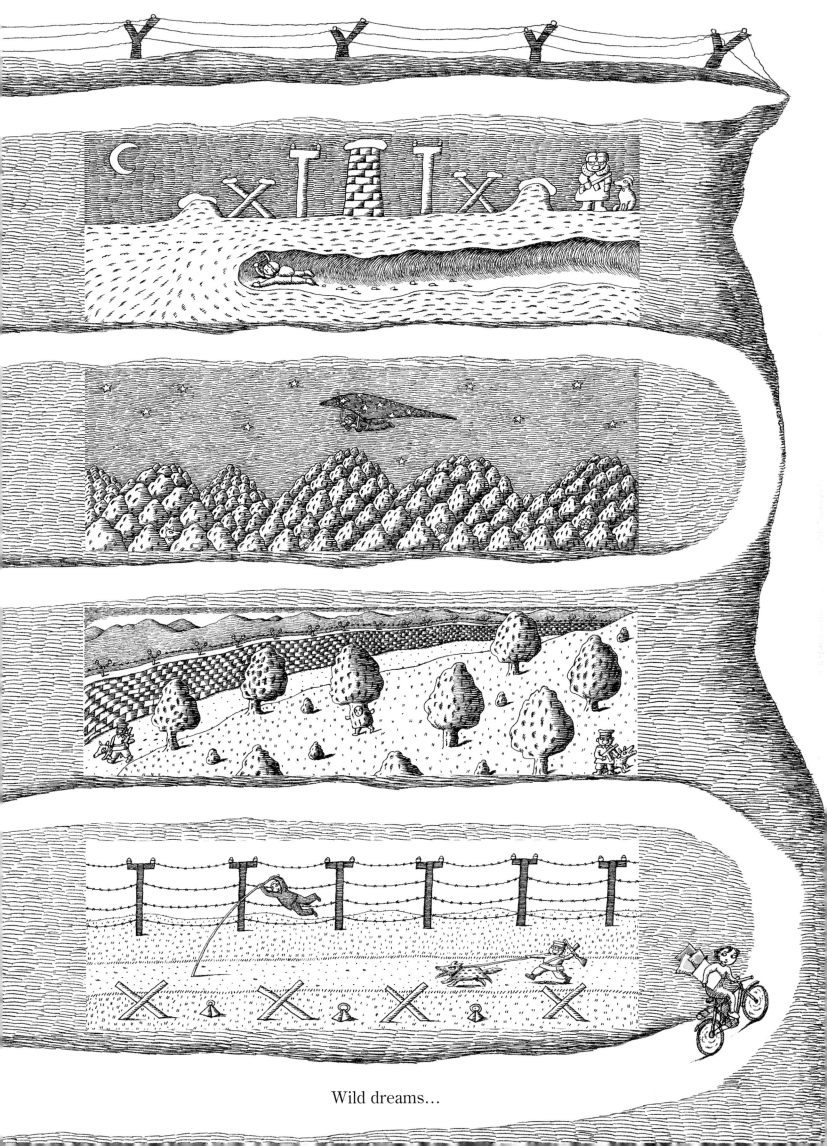

Wild dreams…

HOPE
INSPIRATION
JOY
DREAMS
RESPE
JUSTICE
INTEGRITY
LIBERTY
DIGNITY
TRUTH
FREEDOM
WISDOM
SUSPICION
STUPIDITY
TERROR
FEAR

LOVE

BENEVOLENCE

SPIRIT

PRIDE

ART

HONOR

MORALITY

VIRTUE

TRUST

HAPPINESS

KNOWLEDGE

EQUALITY

INJUSTICE

CORRUPTION

ENVY

LIES

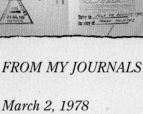

FROM MY JOURNALS

March 2, 1978
Remek blasted off into space.
The first Czech astronaut.

Somebody from England saw my film about alarm clocks at the Krakow festival. I've been offered a scholarship to study at the Royal Academy of Arts. After days of visiting every office in town I finally get permission to go to London. I've been working on a new film for many months, I think I will call it "Heads".

October 1979
Václav Havel is sent to prison for four years for "subversion of the republic".

1980
Heads won best short film, the Golden Bear award, at the West Berlin film festival.
I am trying to get a two-day exit visa, and find myself promising some official that I'll buy hair clippers for her terrier. I end up running from one end of Berlin to the other, looking for the clippers, and therefore I miss my own screening. Nobody knows what happened to the Bear statue.

A letter arrived for me and it looked like it had been opened.

David is my brother. He's 13 years younger than me and goes to school just outside Prague. He's putting together an exhibition in the cellar of our house with some friends from school. They don't have official permission to do this. A special police unit arrives and arrests them.

I'm designing costumes for the opera "The Garrulous Snail".

I break up with Eva.

December 8, 1980
John Lennon has been shot.

July 1982
I've been offered a job by the Olympic committee. Seeing as I am the new young hope of Czech animation, I've been given permission to leave the country for three months. They have invited animators from different countries to film animated promos for various sports. They give me Rowing.

I'm in America.
Hollywood. Palms and pools.
MTV heard that I won a prize. They want me to do a music video of Bob Dylan.
I can't believe it! I'm going to be working on two films at once.

Disaster. The Soviet Union and a few other socialist countries have decided to boycott the Los Angeles Olympics (in retaliation for the boycott of the Moscow Olympics four years earlier?). I got a telegram telling me I should return home IMMEDIATELY. What now? I have to finish the Dylan film, then I'll explain.

1983
The Czechoslovak embassy (comrade Slezáková) is URGING me to return immediately to Prague. If my film is a success, I'll be famous and maybe they won't lock me up.

They didn't like my clip at MTV at all!!
What now?

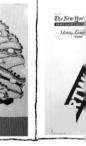

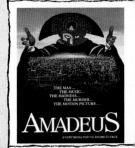

1984

I'm afraid to go home. I'm going around Hollywood showing people my films and drawings. Nobody is interested. Apparently I could illustrate children's books. I should go to New York , where all the publishers are. But how am I going to get there without any money?

Good fortune in the midst of misfortune. Miloš Forman is finishing his film "Amadeus". He's a friend of my father's and he likes my drawings. He's letting me do the poster.
The film was shot in Prague and my house was used as the set for the mask rental store. I'm drawing Prague in Hollywood.
I buy an old car with money I get for the poster, and drive all the way across America without a map.
In Texas I ask a policeman the way to New York. I think I scared him.

New York looks menacing.
I'm staying with a friend of mine, Tomáš, in a one-room studio.

I won't leave Manhattan until I've found a job! I'm doing the rounds of all the editors here. So many editors. Day in and day out.

June 24, 1984
Good news! My first illustration came out today in the New York Times.

1986
My brother fell off the roof in Nerudova trying to look at Halley's comet. He had taken the telescope with him. He is in the hospital, badly hurt, and I can't go see him…

1987
After working intensively for weeks, I finished writing and illustrating my first book. It's called Rainbow Rhino. It is chosen as one the "ten best illustrated books" by the New York Times. I am ecstatic!!!

Finally I can go home with proof that I accomplished something!!!
But it's too late.
My mother informs me that two comrades came to confiscate my things. That means I'm considered a defector. An emigrant.

June 1987
President Reagan came to West Berlin and said, "Tear down this wall!"

1989
The whole of Eastern Europe is in revolt. The news from Malá Strana and Prague is about abandoned trabants and thousands of East Germans in the garden of the West German embassy. They have had enough.

November 17, 1989
Police and students clash on Narodní třída in Prague.
Demonstrations on Wenceslas square.
People jangling their keys.
Václav Havel.
The whole country is waking up.

I'm flying home.
We're finally going to be together again.
The whole family.

In the mid-1980s, Mikhail Gorbachev recognizes the need to open up the rigid Soviet system and introduces the policies of perestroika (restructuring) and glasnost (openness).

SOMETIMES DREAMS COME TRUE

ON NOVEMBER 9, 1989, THE WALL FELL.

"Dad, so what happened to that boy?"

"I think he's still drawing… Now let's go home and we'll paint music…
music full of colors."

There are some things you can experience only once.
The first Beach Boys concert was a wonderful promise of freedom, a taste of America
in occupied Prague in 1969. The second time, we left before the end.
The music was different. The magic was gone.
We are, after all, free to decide what we like and what we don't.

My ten-year old son Matěj came home from school and told me what he had been
learning about American 'settlers'. He asked me how I came to be a settler,
and whether I was one of the good settlers or the bad ones.
I tried to explain with the help of some drawings…

The wall which for many years divided Berlin and the whole of Europe is now, fortunately,
only a memory. But some memories need to be preserved. As a message about the past.
As a warning to the future. Even though one wall has fallen, others remain and more are
being built. All over the world. In Israel, Korea, or on the Mexican border. Symbolic walls,
ideological walls and real walls. Walls of fear, confinement and suspicion.
Walls without which our lives could be freer and happier.